contents

D1428535

British & North American Readers:
Please note that Australian cup and
spoon measurements are metric. A quick
conversion guide appears on page 63.
A glossary explaining unfamiliar terms
and ingredients begins on page 60.

2 tricks of the trade

Having made your favourite cafe treat at home, you know the taste is spot on. But what of the presentation? Read on for techniques that will turn the ordinary-looking into the spectacular.

Dragging a sharp knife over surface of chocolate

striped chocolate curls

For this technique, you will need to choose two chocolate colours. We used white chocolate in these pictures – plain for the first colour and tinted pink for the second. Tint 1 cup (150g) melted white chocolate Melts with rose-pink colouring. Spread chocolate onto cold surface (such as marble); drag a pastry comb through unset chocolate, leave about 5 minutes or until almost set. Spread 1 cup (150g) melted white chocolate Melts over pink chocolate. When chocolate is set, drag a sharp knife over the surface of the chocolate to make curls.

chocolate waves

Secure a sheet of baking paper around a small rolling pin or piece of dowelling. Using a paper piping bag, pipe ³/₄ cup (110g) melted dark chocolate Melts back and forth over paper, forming chocolate waves. Allow to set before peeling chocolate waves off paper.

Allowing chocolate waves to set

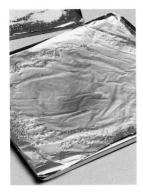

Allowing melted sugar to cool

Peeling toffee from foil

Dragging ice-cream scoop over chocolate

toffee bark

Cover an oven tray with foil, lightly coat foil with cooking-oil spray. Sprinkle evenly with 1/4 cup (55g) sugar. Place under hot grill for about 2 minutes or until sugar is dissolved and golden brown; cool. Carefully peel toffee away from foil, break into pieces. Repeat process to create as much toffee bark as required.

chocolate rosettes

Combine 1/2 teaspoon vegetable oil with 1 cup (150g) melted dark chocolate Melts in small bowl. Spread chocolate onto a cold surface (such as marble); when set, drag an ice-cream scoop over the surface of chocolate to make curls. Repeat process to create as many chocolate rosettes as required.

Painting fruit evenly with egg white

frosted fruit

Choose the quantity of fruit you require; this method works well with strawberries, blueberries, cherries, grapes, even mint leaves and rose petals. Lightly beat one egg white; using a small artist's paintbrush, coat each piece of fruit evenly and sparingly with egg white. Dip wet fruit in a small bowl containing caster sugar. Place frosted fruit on tray lined with baking paper. Leave about 1 hour or until sugar is dry.

4 mississippi mud cake

250g butter, chopped

150g dark chocolate, chopped coarsely

2 cups (440g) caster sugar

1 cup (250ml) hot water

1/3 cup (80ml) Tia Maria or Kahlua

1 tablespoon instant coffee powder

1 1/2 cups (225g) plain flour

1/4 cup (35g) self-raising flour

1/4 cup (25g) cocoa powder

2 eggs

Preheat oven to moderately slow. Grease deep 20cm-round cake pan; line base and side with baking paper.

Combine butter, chocolate, sugar, the water, liqueur and coffee powder in medium saucepan; stir over low heat until chocolate is melted. Transfer mixture to large bowl; cool. Stir in sifted flours and cocoa, then eggs, one at a time; pour mixture into prepared pan.

Bake in moderately slow oven for 1 1/2 hours. Stand cake 30 minutes; turn onto wire rack to cool.

SERVES 16
Per serving 16.7g fat; 1491kJ

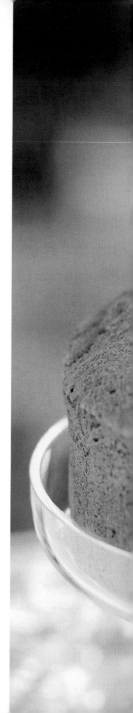

6 plum and cinnamon friands

2 medium plums (200g)
185g butter, melted
1 cup (125g) almond meal
6 egg whites, beaten lightly
1½ cups (240g) icing sugar mixture
½ cup (75g) plain flour
1½ teaspoons ground cinnamon

Preheat oven to moderately hot. Grease 12-hole (1/3 cup/80ml) muffin pan.
Halve plums; discard stones. Cut each half into three wedges. Place butter,
almond meal, egg whites, and sifted icing sugar, flour and cinnamon in
medium bowl; stir until just combined. Divide mixture among pan holes.
Place a plum wedge in each friand. Bake in moderately hot oven about
25 minutes; stand in pan 5 minutes. Turn onto wire rack to cool.

MAKES 12
Per serving 18.5g fat; 1191kJ

panettone and

butter pudding

1kg panettone

90g butter, softened

3 cups (750ml) milk

300ml cream

1/2 cup (110g) caster sugar

5cm piece vanilla bean, split

2 egg yolks

3 eggs

1/4 cup (80g) apricot jam

1 tablespoon Grand Marnier

Preheat oven to moderately slow. Grease deep 23cm round cake pan, line base and side with baking paper.

Halve panettone lengthways, reserve half for another use. Halve lengthways again, then crossways into 1.5cm slices. Toast panettone lightly on both sides; spread one side with butter while still warm. Slightly overlap the slices around sides of prepared pan; layer remaining slices in centre.

Combine milk, cream, sugar and vanilla bean in medium saucepan; stir over heat until mixture comes to a boil. Strain into a jug. Cover; cool 10 minutes.

Whisk egg yolks and eggs in medium bowl until combined, then whisk in milk mixture. Pour the custard over the bread in pan. Place the cake pan in a baking dish, add enough boiling water to come halfway up side of pan.

Bake, uncovered, in moderately slow oven about 1¼ hours or until set in centre. Remove pan from water; stand 30 minutes before turning out.

Brush combined jam and liqueur over warm pudding.

SERVES 8

Per serving 48.7g fat; 3098kJ

8 baklava

1½ cups (165g)
hazelnut meal

1 cup (125g) finely
chopped hazelnuts

⅓ cup (75g)
caster sugar

1 teaspoon
ground cinnamon

180g ghee, melted

12 sheets fillo pastry

orange syrup

1 cup (220g)
caster sugar

⅔ cup (160ml) water

1 teaspoon finely
grated orange rind

½ teaspoon
ground cinnamon

Preheat oven to moderate.
Combine all the nuts, sugar and cinnamon in medium bowl.
Grease 20cm x 30cm lamington pan with a little of the ghee. Layer three of the pastry sheets together, brushing each with a little more ghee. Fold layered sheets in half, press into pan. Sprinkle with a third of the nut mixture.
Continue layering with remaining pastry, more ghee and nut mixture, ending with pastry. Trim pastry edge to fit pan. Cut five strips lengthways through layered pastry, cut each strip into five diamonds. Pour over any remaining ghee.
Bake in moderate oven 30 minutes, reduce heat to slow; bake about 10 minutes or until browned.
Pour hot Orange Syrup over hot baklava; cool in pan.
Orange Syrup Combine ingredients in small saucepan; stir over low heat, without boiling, until sugar dissolves. Simmer, uncovered, without stirring, about 5 minutes or until syrupy.

MAKES 25
Per serving 14.5g fat; 839kJ

10 honey **almond** bread

2 egg whites
$^{1}/_{4}$ cup (55g) caster sugar
1 tablespoon honey
$^{3}/_{4}$ cup (110g) plain flour
$^{1}/_{2}$ teaspoon mixed spice
$^{1}/_{2}$ cup (80g) almond kernels

Preheat oven to moderate. Grease 8cm x 26cm bar cake pan; line base and long sides of pan with baking paper, extending paper 2cm above edge.
Beat egg whites, sugar and honey in small bowl with electric mixer until sugar dissolves. Fold in sifted flour and spice, then nuts; spread mixture into prepared pan.
Bake in moderate oven about 30 minutes or until browned lightly. Cool in pan, wrap in foil; stand overnight.
Using serrated knife, slice bread very thinly. Place slices on baking-paper-lined oven trays; bake, uncovered, in slow oven about 15 minutes or until crisp.

MAKES 50
Per serving 0.9g fat; 98kJ

fig jam and raisin rolls

125g butter

½ cup (100g) firmly
packed brown sugar

2 eggs

1½ cups (225g)
self-raising flour

½ cup (160g) fig jam

1 cup (170g) coarsely
chopped raisins

½ cup (125ml) milk

Preheat oven to moderate.
Grease two 8cm x 17cm nut
roll tins and lids; place one
lid on each tin.

Beat butter and sugar in
small bowl with electric
mixer until light and fluffy.

Add eggs, one at a time,
beating until just combined
between additions. Stir in
flour, jam, raisins and milk,
in two batches. Spoon
cake mixture into prepared
tins; place remaining lids
on tins, stand tins upright
on oven tray.

Bake in moderate oven about
1 hour. Stand rolls in tins
10 minutes; turn onto wire
rack. Serve warm or cold.

SERVES 12
Per serving 10.2g fat; 1107kJ

12 carrot cake

You will need about six medium carrots for this recipe.

1 cup (250ml) vegetable oil

1⅓ cups (250g) firmly packed brown sugar

3 eggs

3 cups (720g) firmly packed, coarsely grated carrot

1 cup (120g) coarsely chopped walnuts

2½ cups (375g) self-raising flour

½ teaspoon bicarbonate of soda

2 teaspoons mixed spice

lemon cream cheese frosting

30g butter

80g cream cheese, softened

1 teaspoon finely grated lemon rind

1½ cups (240g) icing sugar mixture

Preheat oven to moderate. Grease deep 23cm-round cake pan, line base with baking paper.

Beat oil, sugar and eggs in small bowl with electric mixer until thick and creamy. Transfer mixture to large bowl, stir in carrot and nuts, then sifted dry ingredients.

Pour mixture into prepared pan, bake in moderate oven about 1¼ hours. Cover cake loosely with foil halfway through cooking. Stand cake 5 minutes; turn onto wire rack to cool. Spread Lemon Cream Cheese Frosting over cold cake.

Lemon Cream Cheese Frosting Beat butter, cream cheese and rind in small bowl with electric mixer until light and fluffy; gradually beat in icing sugar.

SERVES 12
Per serving 32.1g fat; 2377kJ

14 pecan and

macadamia pie

Blend or process flour, icing sugar and butter until crumbly; add egg yolk and juice, process until ingredients just come together. Knead gently on floured surface until smooth, wrap dough in plastic wrap; refrigerate 30 minutes.

Roll dough between sheets of baking paper until large enough to line a 24cm-round loose-base flan tin. Lift pastry into tin; ease into side, trim edge. Cover; refrigerate 30 minutes.

Preheat oven to moderately hot. Cover pastry with baking paper, fill with dried beans or rice, place on oven tray. Bake in moderately hot oven 15 minutes. Remove paper and beans; bake about 10 minutes or until pastry is browned lightly, cool. Place both nuts in pastry shell. Pour Filling over nuts; bake in moderate oven 30 minutes or until set.

Filling Combine sugar, flour, butter and eggs in medium bowl; gradually whisk in maple syrup.

SERVES 8
Per serving 43.1g fat; 2720kJ

1 1/4 cups (185g) plain flour

1/3 cup (55g) icing sugar mixture

125g cold butter, chopped coarsely

1 egg yolk

2 teaspoons lemon juice

1 1/4 cups (155g) coarsely chopped toasted pecans

1/2 cup (75g) coarsely chopped toasted macadamias

filling

1/4 cup (50g) firmly packed brown sugar

1 tablespoon plain flour

60g butter, melted

3 eggs

1 cup (250ml) maple syrup

spicy date and pecan cookies

185g butter, chopped

2 teaspoons
vanilla essence

1/2 cup (110g)
caster sugar

1 egg yolk

1 1/2 cups (225g)
self-raising flour

1 teaspoon
ground cinnamon

1/2 teaspoon
ground nutmeg

2/3 cup (110g) coarsely
chopped seeded dates

1/2 cup (50g) pecans,
chopped coarsely

2/3 cup (70g)
pecan halves

Beat butter, essence, sugar and egg yolk in small bowl with electric mixer until light and fluffy. Stir in sifted flour and spices, then dates and chopped pecans; refrigerate 30 minutes.

Preheat oven to moderately hot. Roll rounded teaspoons of mixture into balls, place 4cm apart on greased oven trays. Top with pecan halves. Bake in moderately hot oven 12 minutes or until browned lightly; cool on trays.

MAKES 50
Per serving 4.9g fat; 314kJ

16 white chocolate

mud cake

250g butter, chopped

150g white chocolate, chopped coarsely

2 cups (440g) caster sugar

1 cup (250ml) milk

1½ cups (225g) plain flour

½ cup (75g) self-raising flour

1 teaspoon vanilla essence

2 eggs, beaten lightly

white chocolate ganache

½ cup (125ml) cream

300g white chocolate, chopped coarsely

Grease deep 20cm-round cake pan; line base and side with baking paper.
Combine butter, chocolate, sugar and milk in medium saucepan; stir over low heat, without boiling, until smooth. Transfer mixture to large bowl; cool 15 minutes.
Preheat oven to moderately slow.
Whisk sifted flours into mixture, then stir in essence and eggs. Pour mixture into prepared pan; bake in moderately slow oven 1 hour. Cover pan with foil; bake about 45 minutes.
Stand cake in pan 30 minutes; turn onto wire rack to cool. Spread top and side of cold cake with white chocolate ganache.
White Chocolate Ganache Bring cream to a boil in small saucepan; pour over chocolate in small bowl, stirring until chocolate melts. Cover; refrigerate, stirring occasionally, about 30 minutes or until spreadable.

SERVES 12
Per serving 36.1g fat; 2706kJ

18 chocolate
chip cookies

125g butter, chopped

1 teaspoon
vanilla essence

*1/3 cup (75g) firmly
packed brown sugar*

*1/3 cup (75g)
caster sugar*

1 egg

*1 1/4 cups (185g)
plain flour*

*1/2 teaspoon
bicarbonate of soda*

*1/4 cup (30g)
finely chopped
walnuts, toasted*

*1 cup (190g) dark
Choc Bits*

Preheat oven to moderately hot.

Beat butter, essence, sugars and egg in small bowl with electric mixer until smooth. Stir in sifted dry ingredients, nuts and Choc Bits. Drop level tablespoons of mixture about 5cm apart on greased oven trays, press down lightly. Bake in moderately hot oven 12 minutes or until browned lightly. Stand cookies 2 minutes before lifting onto wire racks to cool.

MAKES 25
Per serving 7.4g fat; 566kJ

rhubarb cake

60g butter

1 teaspoon finely
grated lemon rind

1½ cups (300g) firmly
packed brown sugar

2 eggs

1 cup (150g)
self-raising flour

1 cup (150g) plain flour

1 teaspoon
ground cinnamon

1 cup (240g)
sour cream

6 cups (500g) fresh
rhubarb, trimmed,
chopped coarsely

⅓ cup (75g) firmly
packed brown
sugar, extra

1 teaspoon ground
cinnamon, extra

Preheat oven to moderate. Grease deep 23cm-round cake pan, line
base with baking paper.
Beat butter, rind, sugar and eggs in medium bowl with electric mixer until
light and fluffy (mixture may curdle). Stir in sifted flours and cinnamon
and cream, in two batches; stir in rhubarb. Spread cake mixture into
prepared pan; sprinkle with combined extra sugar and extra cinnamon.
Bake in moderate oven about 1½ hours. Stand cake in pan 5 minutes;
turn onto wire rack to cool.

SERVES 10
Per serving 16g fat; 1650kJ

20 banana cake with passionfruit icing

You will need about 3 medium overripe bananas (600g) for this recipe.

125g butter

³/₄ cup (150g) firmly packed brown sugar

1 teaspoon mixed spice

2 eggs

1¹/₂ cups (225g) self-raising flour

¹/₂ teaspoon bicarbonate of soda

1 cup mashed banana

¹/₂ cup (120g) sour cream

¹/₄ cup (60ml) milk

passionfruit icing

1¹/₂ cups (240g) icing sugar mixture

1 teaspoon soft butter

2 tablespoons passionfruit pulp, approximately

Preheat oven to moderate. Grease 15cm x 25cm loaf pan, line base with baking paper.

Beat butter, sugar and spice in small bowl with electric mixer until light and fluffy. Beat in eggs one at a time until combined. Transfer mixture to large bowl, stir in sifted flour and soda with remaining ingredients.

Spread mixture into prepared pan; bake in moderate oven about 50 minutes. Stand cake in pan 5 minutes; turn onto wire rack to cool. Spread cold cake with Passionfruit Icing.

Passionfruit Icing Place icing sugar in small heatproof bowl, stir in butter and enough pulp to give a firm paste. Stir over hot water until icing is spreadable; do not overheat.

SERVES 10
Per serving 17.1g fat; 1691kJ

22 greek almond
biscuits

3 cups (375g)
almond meal

1 cup (220g)
caster sugar

3 drops almond essence

3 egg whites

1 cup (80g)
flaked almonds

Preheat oven to moderate.
Combine almond meal,
sugar and essence in
large bowl. Add egg
whites; stir until mixture
forms a firm paste.
Roll level tablespoons
of mixture into the
flaked almonds, then
roll into 8cm logs.
Press on the remaining
almonds. Shape logs
to form crescents.
Place on baking-paper-
lined oven trays; bake
in moderate oven
about 15 minutes or
until browned lightly.
Cool on trays.

MAKES 25
Per serving 10.1g fat; 597kJ

portuguese
custard tarts

3 egg yolks

½ cup (110g) caster sugar

2 tablespoons cornflour

¾ cup (180ml) cream

½ cup (125ml) water

strip of lemon rind

2 teaspoons vanilla essence

1 sheet frozen ready-rolled puff pastry

Preheat oven to hot. Grease 12-hole (⅓ cup/80ml) muffin pan.
Whisk egg yolks, sugar and cornflour in medium saucepan until combined. Gradually whisk in cream and water until smooth. Add lemon rind; stir over medium heat until mixture boils and thickens. Remove pan from heat, remove and discard rind; stir in essence. Cover surface of custard with plastic wrap, cool.
Cut pastry sheet in half. Stack the two halves on top of each other. Stand about 5 minutes or until thawed. Roll the pastry up tightly from the short side, then cut the log into twelve 1cm rounds. Lay pastry, cut-side up, on a floured surface; roll each round out to about 10cm. Press rounds into the prepared muffin pans with your fingers.
Spoon cooled custard into pastry cases. Bake in hot oven 20 minutes or until browned well. Stand tarts 5 minutes; transfer to wire rack to cool.

MAKES 12
Per serving 11.1g fat; 704kJ

24 sacher torte

100g dark chocolate, chopped coarsely

1 cup (250ml) water

125g butter, chopped

1¼ cups (250g) firmly packed brown sugar

3 eggs

1 cup (150g) self-raising flour

¼ cup (25g) cocoa powder

½ cup (60g) almond meal

⅓ cup (110g) apricot jam

ganache

200g dark chocolate, chopped coarsely

⅔ cup (160ml) cream

Preheat oven to moderately slow. Grease deep 23cm-round cake pan, line base with baking paper.

Combine chocolate and the water in small saucepan, stir over low heat until chocolate is melted; cool.

Beat butter and sugar in small bowl with electric mixer until combined; beat in eggs, one at a time, beating well between additions. Transfer mixture to large bowl, stir in sifted flour and cocoa, almond meal and chocolate mixture.

Pour mixture into prepared pan. Bake in moderately slow oven about 1 hour and 10 minutes. Stand cake 10 minutes; turn onto wire rack to cool.

Split cold cake in half; sandwich with jam. Place cake on wire rack over tray. Spread cake all over with a thin layer of Ganache. Heat remaining Ganache over hot water until pourable (do not overheat). Strain Ganache, pour over cake; working quickly, smooth top and side of cake. Allow ganache to set at room temperature.

Ganache Place chocolate and cream in small heatproof bowl over saucepan of simmering water, stir until chocolate is melted.

SERVES 12
Per serving 26.5g fat; 1893kJ

new york
cheesecake

250g packet plain
sweet biscuits

125g butter, melted

750g packaged
cream cheese

3 eggs

1 cup (220g)
caster sugar

¾ cup (180g)
sour cream

2 teaspoons finely
grated lemon rind

¼ cup (60ml)
lemon juice

Line base of 22cm springform tin with foil. Process biscuits until
finely crushed, add butter; process until combined.
Press biscuit mixture over base and side of prepared tin. Place
tin on oven tray; refrigerate 30 minutes.
Preheat oven to moderately slow.
Beat the remaining ingredients in medium bowl with electric mixer until
smooth. Pour cheese mixture into biscuit crust. Bake in moderately slow
oven about 1 hour or until just set in centre. Turn oven off, cool cheesecake
in oven with door ajar. Cover; refrigerate cheesecake overnight. Serve
with fresh figs if desired.
SERVES 12
Per serving 41.7g fat; 2239kJ

lemon tart

*You will need about three
lemons for this recipe.*

1¼ cups (185g) plain flour

⅓ cup (55g) icing
sugar mixture

¼ cup (30g) almond meal

125g butter, chopped coarsely

1 egg yolk

lemon filling

1 tablespoon finely
grated lemon rind

½ cup (125ml) lemon juice

5 eggs

¾ cup (165g) caster sugar

1 cup (250ml) thickened cream

Blend or process flour, sugar, almond meal and butter until combined; add
egg yolk, process until ingredients just come together. Knead on floured
surface until smooth, wrap dough in plastic wrap; refrigerate 30 minutes.
Roll dough between sheets of baking paper until large enough to line
24cm-round loose-base flan tin. Lift pastry into tin, ease into side, trim
edge. Cover; refrigerate 1 hour.
Preheat oven to moderately hot. Cover pastry with baking paper, fill with
dried beans or rice, place on oven tray. Bake in moderately hot oven
15 minutes. Remove paper and beans, bake about 10 minutes or until
pastry is browned lightly; cool. Pour Lemon Filling into pastry case; bake
in moderate oven about 30 minutes or until filling has set slightly, cool.
Cover; refrigerate until cold.
Decorate with thin slices of lemon that have been cooked until
translucent in sugar syrup, and serve with thick cream, if desired.
Lemon Filling Whisk ingredients in medium bowl; stand 5 minutes.
SERVES 8
Per serving 30.7g fat; 2042kJ

28 baked honey and
cinnamon cheesecake

1½ cups (225g)
plain flour

125g cold butter,
chopped coarsely

¼ cup (55g)
caster sugar

1 egg yolk

2 tablespoons finely
grated lemon rind

3 teaspoons cold
water, approximately

cheesecake filling

1¼ cups (250g)
cottage cheese

250g packaged
cream cheese

¾ cup (265g) honey

½ cup (110g)
caster sugar

2 teaspoons
ground cinnamon

4 eggs

Grease 22cm springform tin.

Place flour in medium bowl, rub in butter. Add sugar, egg yolk, rind and enough of the water to make ingredients cling together. Knead gently on floured surface until smooth, wrap dough in plastic wrap; refrigerate 30 minutes.

Roll dough between sheets of baking paper until large enough to line prepared tin. Lift pastry into tin, ease into side, trim edge. Cover; refrigerate 30 minutes.

Preheat oven to moderately hot. Cover pastry with baking paper, fill with dried beans or rice, place on oven tray. Bake in moderately hot oven 10 minutes. Remove paper and beans; bake about 10 minutes or until pastry is browned lightly, cool.

Pour Cheesecake Filling into pastry case; bake in moderately slow oven about 1½ hours or until filling is firm, cool. Cover; refrigerate cheesecake overnight. Just before serving, drizzle with a little extra honey, if desired.

Cheesecake Filling Beat cheeses, honey, sugar and cinnamon in medium bowl with electric mixer until almost smooth. Add eggs, one at a time, beating well after each addition.

SERVES 8
Per serving 28.7g fat; 2451kJ

30 pear crumble cake

It is important to slice pears as thinly as possible. If the slices are too thick, the cake will sink in the centre.

2 cups (500ml) water

1 cup (220g) caster sugar

2 cinnamon sticks

2 small (360g) pears, sliced thinly

125g butter

2/3 cup (150g) caster sugar, extra

2 eggs

1 1/2 cups (225g) self-raising flour

crumble topping

1/2 cup (75g) plain flour

1/3 cup (75g) caster sugar

60g butter

1/2 cup (45g) desiccated coconut

Line base and side of 22cm springform tin with foil.

Combine the water, sugar and cinnamon in large frying pan; stir over heat, without boiling, until sugar dissolves. Add pears; simmer, uncovered, about 5 minutes or until just tender, drain on absorbent paper.
Preheat oven to moderate.

Beat butter and extra sugar in small bowl with electric mixer until light and fluffy. Add eggs, one at a time, beating until just combined between additions. Add flour; beat on low speed until just combined, spread into prepared tin.

Top cake mixture with half the pears, sprinkle with half the Crumble Topping; repeat with remaining pears and Topping. Bake in moderate oven 1 hour. Cool cake in tin.

Crumble Topping Blend or process ingredients until fine and crumbly.

SERVES 10
Per serving 19.5g fat; 1962kJ

When it comes to a fast, easy and popular treat, the muffin wins hands down. So feast your eyes on these tasty little numbers.

choc chip muffins

2½ cups (375g) self-raising flour

90g butter, chopped

1 cup (220g) caster sugar

1¼ cups (310ml) buttermilk

1 egg, beaten lightly

1 cup (190g) dark Choc Bits

Preheat oven to moderately hot. Grease a 12-hole (⅓ cup/80ml) muffin pan.

Place flour in large bowl, rub in butter. Stir in sugar, buttermilk, egg and Choc Bits until just combined; do not over-mix. Divide mixture among holes of prepared pan, bake in moderately hot oven about 20 minutes.

Stand muffins in pan 5 minutes; turn onto wire rack to cool.

MAKES 12
per muffin 12.3g fat; 1386kJ

raspberry and coconut muffins

2½ cups (375g) self-raising flour

90g butter, chopped

1 cup (220g) caster sugar

1¼ cups (310ml) buttermilk

1 egg, beaten lightly

⅓ cup (30g) desiccated coconut

150g fresh or frozen raspberries

2 tablespoons shredded coconut

Preheat oven to moderately hot. Grease 12-hole (⅓ cup/80ml) muffin pan.

Place flour in large bowl, rub in butter. Stir in sugar, buttermilk, egg, desiccated coconut and raspberries until just combined; do not over-mix. Divide mixture among holes of prepared pan; sprinkle over shredded coconut. Bake in moderately hot oven about 20 minutes.

Stand muffins in pan 5 minutes; turn onto wire rack to cool.

MAKES 12
per muffin 9.8g fat; 1164kJ

date and pecan muffins

*2¹/₂ cups (375g)
self-raising flour*

90g butter, chopped

1 cup (220g) caster sugar

1¹/₄ cups (310ml) buttermilk

1 egg, beaten lightly

*1 cup (160g) seeded
chopped dates*

*¹/₂ cup (60g) coarsely
chopped pecans*

1 teaspoon ground ginger

12 pecan halves

Preheat oven to moderately hot. Grease 12-hole (¹/₃ cup/80ml) muffin pan.
Place flour in large bowl, rub in butter. Stir in sugar, buttermilk, egg, dates, chopped nuts and ginger until just combined; do not over-mix. Divide mixture among holes of prepared pan, top with pecan halves. Bake in moderately hot oven about 20 minutes.
Stand muffins in pan 5 minutes; turn onto wire rack to cool.

MAKES 12
per muffin 12.7g fat; 1389kJ

*left to right: date and
pecan; raspberry and
coconut; choc chip.*

34 apple cake

185g butter, chopped

2 teaspoons finely
grated orange rind

$^2/_3$ cup (150g)
caster sugar

3 eggs

1 cup (150g)
self-raising flour

$^1/_2$ cup (75g) plain flour

$^1/_3$ cup (80ml) milk

2 medium
apples (300g)

$^1/_3$ cup (90g)
marmalade,
warmed, strained

Preheat oven to moderate.
Grease deep 23cm-round cake
pan; line base with baking paper.
Beat butter, rind and sugar in
medium bowl with electric mixer
until light and fluffy. Beat in eggs,
one at a time, until just combined.
Sift about half of the flours over
butter mixture, add about half
of the milk; stir with a wooden
spoon only until combined. Stir
in remaining sifted flours and
milk until mixture is smooth.
Spread cake mixture evenly
into prepared pan.
Peel, quarter and core apples.
Make several closely placed
cuts in the rounded side of each
apple quarter, slicing about
three-quarters of the way through
each piece. Place quarters,
rounded-side up, around edge
of cake. Bake in moderate oven
about 1 hour or until cooked
when tested.
Stand cake 5 minutes before
turning onto wire rack. Remove
paper, turn cake right way up
onto another rack. Brush warm
marmalade over top of hot cake;
cool before cutting.

SERVES 8
Per serving 21.6g fat; 1721kJ

36 coconut

almond biscotti

1 cup (220g)
caster sugar

2 eggs

1 teaspoon finely
grated orange rind

1¹⁄₃ cups (200g)
plain flour

¹⁄₃ cup (50g)
self-raising flour

²⁄₃ cup (50g)
shredded coconut

1 cup (160g)
blanched almonds

Preheat oven to moderate.

Whisk sugar, eggs and rind in medium bowl. Stir in flours, coconut and nuts; mix to a sticky dough. Divide dough into two portions. Using floured hands, roll each portion into a 20cm log, place on greased oven tray.

Bake in moderate oven about 35 minutes or until browned lightly; cool on tray. Using a serrated knife, cut logs diagonally into 1cm slices. Place slices on oven trays. Bake in moderately slow oven about 25 minutes or until dry and crisp, turning over halfway through baking; cool on trays.

MAKES 30
Per serving 4.5g fat; 433kJ

rock cakes

2 cups (300g)
self-raising flour

¹/₄ teaspoon
ground cinnamon

90g butter

¹/₃ cup (75g)
caster sugar

1 cup (160g) sultanas

2 tablespoons
mixed peel

1 egg, beaten lightly

¹/₂ cup (125ml) milk,
approximately

1 tablespoon caster
sugar, extra

Preheat oven to moderately hot. Place flour and cinnamon in large bowl, rub in butter, stir in sugar and fruit. Stir in egg, then enough milk to give a moist but still firm consistency. Drop rounded tablespoons of mixture about 5cm apart on greased oven trays. Sprinkle cakes with a little extra sugar.
Bake in moderately hot oven about 15 minutes or until browned.
Loosen cakes; cool on trays.

MAKES 18
Per serving 4.9g fat; 636kJ

38 chocolate

meringue torte

6 egg whites

1 cup (220g)
caster sugar

1 cup (140g)
slivered almonds

1/2 cup (95g) mixed
dried fruit

200g dark chocolate,
grated coarsely

1 1/2 cups (300g)
ricotta cheese

3/4 cup (180ml) cream

1/3 cup (80ml) Kahlua
or Tia Maria

**chocolate twists
and curls**

1 cup (150g)
white chocolate
Melts, melted

1 cup (150g)
dark chocolate
Melts, melted

2/3 cup (100g) dark
chocolate Melts,
melted, extra

Preheat oven to moderately slow. Grease 24cm springform tin, line base with foil, grease foil.

Beat egg whites in medium bowl with electric mixer until soft peaks form; gradually add sugar, beating until dissolved after each addition. Fold in nuts, fruit and half of the chocolate. Spoon into prepared tin.

Bake in moderately slow oven about 1 1/4 hours or until firm. Turn oven off, cool meringue in oven with door ajar.

Beat cheese and cream in medium bowl with electric mixer until almost smooth. Stir in liqueur and remaining chocolate. Spread mixture over top and side of meringue, decorate with Chocolate Twists and Curls; dust with sifted cocoa, if desired.

Chocolate Twists and Curls Cut 2cm x 20cm strips of baking paper. Spread chocolates, separately, over baking paper. Wrap strips around wooden spoon handles or dowel, allow to set; peel away paper. Spread extra chocolate in a thin layer on cool surface, allow to just set. Using a large sharp knife at 45-degree angle, pull knife over extra chocolate to form curls.

SERVES 10
Per serving 39g fat; 2724kJ

40 caramel

chocolate slice

1 cup (150g) self-raising flour

1 cup (90g) desiccated coconut

1 cup (200g) firmly packed brown sugar

125g butter, melted

filling

400g can (300ml) sweetened condensed milk

30g butter

2 tablespoons golden syrup

topping

125g dark chocolate, chopped coarsely

30g butter

Preheat oven to moderate. Grease 20cm x 30cm lamington pan.
Combine flour, coconut and sugar in medium bowl;
add butter, stir until combined. Press mixture over base of
prepared pan. Bake in moderate oven 15 minutes.
Pour hot Filling over hot base, return to oven 10 minutes;
cool. Spread warm Topping over Filling, stand at room
temperature until set. Cut into 5cm squares.
Filling Combine milk, butter and golden syrup in small heavy-base
saucepan; stir over heat, without boiling, about 15 minutes
or until mixture is golden brown.
Topping Combine chocolate and butter in small saucepan;
stir over low heat until smooth.

MAKES 24
Per serving 11.9g fat; 905kJ

florentines

½ cup (80g) sultanas

2 cups (60g)
corn flakes

¾ cup (105g)
slivered almonds,
chopped coarsely

½ cup (105g)
glacé cherries,
chopped finely

2 tablespoons finely
chopped glacé ginger

⅔ cup (160ml)
sweetened
condensed milk

250g dark
chocolate, melted

Preheat oven to moderate. Combine sultanas, corn flakes, nuts, cherries, ginger and milk in large bowl. Drop rounded teaspoons of mixture about 2cm apart on baking-paper-lined oven trays.
Bake in moderate oven about 10 minutes or until browned; cool on trays. Spread base of each florentine with chocolate. Make wavy lines in chocolate with fork just before chocolate sets.

MAKES 50
Per serving 3.1g fat; 285kJ

This cake is delicious for afternoon tea or dessert. Try replacing the pistachios with toasted slivered almonds, if you like.

³/₄ cup (110g) caster sugar

¹/₂ cup (125ml) orange juice

1 cup (250ml) water

2 cardamom pods, crushed

3 medium quinces (990g), peeled, cored, sliced

pistachio cake batter

90g butter

2 teaspoons grated orange rind

1 cup (220g) caster sugar

3 eggs

¹/₂ cup (75g) self-raising flour

1 cup (150g) plain flour

¹/₄ teaspoon bicarbonate of soda

¹/₂ cup (125ml) sour cream

¹/₄ cup (60ml) orange juice

¹/₂ cup (75g) chopped toasted pistachios

Combine sugar, juice, the water and cardamom in medium saucepan; stir over heat, without boiling, until sugar is dissolved. Add quince; simmer, uncovered for about 1¼ hours or until quince is soft and liquid is almost absorbed; cool. Remove cardamom pods.

Preheat oven to moderate. Grease deep 23cm-round cake pan; cover base with baking paper.

Arrange two-thirds of the quince over the base of the pan. Blend or process the remaining quince until smooth. Gently fold quince puree into Pistachio Cake Batter to give a rippled effect. Spread cake batter over quince in cake pan.

Bake in moderate oven about 1¼ hours. Stand cake in pan for 15 minutes before turning onto wire rack. Cake can be served hot or at room temperature, with cream, custard or ice-cream, if desired.

Pistachio Cake Batter Beat butter, rind and sugar in small bowl with electric mixer until combined. Beat in eggs, one at a time, until combined (mixture will curdle). Stir in sifted flours and soda, with cream and juice, in two batches. Fold in nuts.

SERVES 10
Per serving 17.8g fat; 1752kJ

44 baked lemon
ricotta cheesecake

1 cup (100g) plain sweet biscuit crumbs

½ cup (60g) almond meal

80g butter, melted

filling

2½ cups (500g) ricotta cheese, sieved

1 cup (250g) mascarpone cheese

⅔ cup (150g) caster sugar

1 tablespoon finely grated lemon rind

¼ teaspoon ground cinnamon

3 eggs

⅓ cup (55g) sultanas

Grease 22cm springform tin, line base and side with baking paper. Combine crumbs, almond meal and butter in medium bowl. Press mixture over base of prepared tin, refrigerate until firm.

Preheat oven to moderately slow.

Pour Filling over base, place tin on oven tray. Bake in moderately slow oven about 1½ hours or until filling is just firm in centre. Turn oven off, cool cheesecake in oven with door ajar. Cover; refrigerate cheesecake overnight.

Filling Beat cheeses, sugar, rind and cinnamon in medium bowl with electric mixer until smooth. Add eggs, beat until just combined. Stir in sultanas.

SERVES 10
Per serving 33.9g fat; 1853kJ

almond and

strawberry friands

*Rectangular or
oval friand pans
are available from
specialty cookware
and kitchen stores.
Muffin pans can
also be used.*

185g butter, melted

*1 cup (125g)
almond meal*

*6 egg whites,
beaten lightly*

*1½ cups (240g) icing
sugar mixture*

½ cup (75g) plain flour

*100g strawberries,
sliced thinly*

Preheat oven to moderately hot. Grease 12 (⅓ cup/80ml) rectangular
or oval friand pans, stand on oven tray.
Combine butter, almond meal, egg whites, sugar and flour in medium
bowl; stir until just combined. Divide mixture among prepared pans;
scatter with strawberry slices. Bake in moderately hot oven about
25 minutes; stand in pans 5 minutes, turn onto wire rack to cool.
Serve dusted with a little extra sifted icing sugar.

MAKES 12
Per serving 18.5g fat; 1174kJ

46 caramel mud cake

185g butter, chopped

150g white chocolate, chopped coarsely

1 cup (200g) firmly packed brown sugar

$1/3$ cup (80ml) golden syrup

1 cup (250ml) milk

$1^1/2$ cups (225g) plain flour

$1/2$ cup (75g) self-raising flour

2 eggs

white chocolate ganache

$1/2$ cup (125ml) cream

300g white chocolate, chopped coarsely

Preheat oven to moderately slow. Grease deep 23cm-round cake pan; line base and side with baking paper.
Combine butter, chocolate, sugar, golden syrup and milk in medium saucepan; stir over low heat, without boiling, until smooth. Transfer mixture to large bowl; cool 15 minutes.
Whisk in sifted flours, then eggs, one at a time. Pour mixture into prepared pan; bake in moderately slow oven about 1 1/2 hours.
Stand cake in pan 30 minutes; turn onto wire rack to cool. Spread top and side with White Chocolate Ganache.
White Chocolate Ganache Bring cream to boil in small saucepan; pour over chocolate in small bowl, stirring until chocolate melts. Cover; refrigerate, stirring occasionally, about 30 minutes or until spreadable.

SERVES 12
Per serving 31.6g fat; 2321kJ

48 carrot

and banana cake

You will need about
4 medium carrots
(480g) and 2 large
overripe bananas
(460g) for this recipe.

1¼ cups (185g)
plain flour

½ cup (75g)
self-raising flour

1 teaspoon
bicarbonate of soda

1 teaspoon
mixed spice

½ teaspoon
ground cinnamon

1 cup (200g) firmly
packed brown sugar

¾ cup (90g) coarsely
chopped walnuts
or pecans

3 eggs, beaten lightly

2 cups finely
grated carrot

1 cup mashed banana

1 cup (250ml)
vegetable oil

Preheat oven to moderately slow. Grease 24cm
springform tin, line base with baking paper.
Sift flours, soda, spices and sugar into large
bowl, stir in remaining ingredients; pour cake
mixture into prepared tin. Bake in moderately
slow oven about 1¼ hours. Cool cake in tin.

SERVES 10
Per serving 31.4g fat; 2055kJ

orange poppyseed

syrup cake

1/3 cup (50g) poppyseeds

1/4 cup (60ml) milk

185g butter, chopped

1 tablespoon finely grated orange rind

1 cup (220g) caster sugar

3 eggs

1 1/2 cups (225g) self-raising flour

1/2 cup (75g) plain flour

1/2 cup (60g) almond meal

1/2 cup (125ml) orange juice

orange syrup

1 cup (220g) caster sugar

2/3 cup (160ml) orange juice

1/3 cup (80ml) water

Grease deep 23cm-round cake pan, line base and side with baking paper. Combine seeds and milk in small bowl, stand 20 minutes. Preheat oven to moderate.
Beat butter, rind and sugar in small bowl with electric mixer until light and fluffy; beat in eggs one at a time, beat until combined. Transfer mixture to large bowl, stir in sifted flours, almond meal, juice and poppyseed mixture.
Spread into prepared pan; bake in moderate oven about 55 minutes. Stand cake 5 minutes. Turn cake onto wire rack over tray, pour hot Orange Syrup over hot cake. Pour any syrup in tray into jug, pour back over cake.
Orange Syrup Combine ingredients in small saucepan, stir over heat, without boiling, until sugar is dissolved. Simmer, uncovered, without stirring, 2 minutes.

SERVES 16
Per serving 14.3g fat; 1310kJ

50 hummingbird

cake

You will need about 2 large (460g) overripe bananas for this recipe.

450g can crushed pineapple in syrup

1 cup (150g) plain flour

1/2 cup (75g) self-raising flour

1/2 teaspoon bicarbonate of soda

1/2 teaspoon ground cinnamon

1/2 teaspoon ground ginger

1 cup (200g) firmly packed brown sugar

1/2 cup (45g) desiccated coconut

1 cup mashed banana

2 eggs, beaten lightly

3/4 cup (180ml) vegetable oil

cream cheese frosting

60g cream cheese, softened

30g butter

1 teaspoon vanilla essence

1 1/2 cups (240g) icing sugar mixture

Preheat oven to moderate. Grease 23cm-square slab cake pan, line base with baking paper.
Drain pineapple over medium bowl; reserve 1/4 cup (60ml) syrup.
Sift flours, soda, spices and sugar into large bowl. Stir in pineapple, reserved syrup, coconut, banana, eggs and oil. Pour into prepared pan; bake in moderate oven about 50 minutes. Stand cake 5 minutes; turn onto wire rack to cool. Spread cold cake with Cream Cheese Frosting.
Decorate cake with fresh flowers, if desired; remove flowers to serve.

Cream Cheese Frosting
Beat cream cheese, butter and essence in small bowl with electric mixer until light and fluffy; gradually beat in icing sugar.

SERVES 12
Per serving 21.1g fat; 1853kJ

52 chocolate brownies

30g butter

250g dark chocolate, chopped finely

80g butter, extra

2 teaspoons vanilla essence

1 cup (200g) firmly packed brown sugar

2 eggs

½ cup (75g) plain flour

½ cup (60g) coarsely chopped roasted hazelnuts

⅓ cup (80g) sour cream

chocolate icing

125g dark chocolate, chopped coarsely

60g unsalted butter

Preheat oven to moderate. Grease deep 19cm square cake pan, line base with baking paper; grease paper. Melt butter in small saucepan, add chocolate; stir over low heat until chocolate melts, cool 5 minutes.
Beat extra butter, essence and sugar in small bowl with electric mixer until light and fluffy; beat in eggs one at a time. Transfer mixture to large bowl. Stir in sifted flour, then chocolate mixture, nuts and cream.
Spread mixture into prepared pan. Bake in moderate oven about 45 minutes; cool in pan. Turn slice onto board, remove paper. Spread cold slice with Chocolate Icing; cut when set.
Chocolate Icing Melt chocolate and butter in small heatproof bowl over simmering water; cool to room temperature. Beat with wooden spoon until thick and spreadable.

MAKES 16
Per serving 20.5g fat; 1310kJ

date and walnut rolls

1 cup (180g) finely chopped seeded dates

60g butter

1 cup (200g) firmly packed brown sugar

1 cup (250ml) water

2 cups (300g) self-raising flour

1/2 teaspoon bicarbonate of soda

1/2 cup (65g) coarsely chopped walnuts

1 egg, beaten lightly

Preheat oven to moderate. Grease two 8cm x 19cm nut roll tins, line bases with baking paper. Place tins upright on oven tray.
Combine dates, butter, sugar and the water in small saucepan, stir over heat, without boiling, until sugar is dissolved. Bring to a boil, remove from heat; cool.
Sift flour and soda into medium bowl, stir in date mixture, nuts and egg. Spoon mixture into prepared tins, place lids on tins.
Bake in moderate oven about 50 minutes. Stand rolls 5 minutes before removing lids and turning onto wire rack to cool.

SERVES 24
Per serving 4.3g fat; 512kJ

54 citrus almond

syrup cake

2 small
oranges (360g)

1½ cups (240g)
almond kernels

1 cup (220g)
caster sugar

6 eggs

1 teaspoon
baking powder

1 teaspoon
vanilla essence

lime syrup

½ cup (110g)
caster sugar

¼ cup (60ml)
lime juice

¼ cup (60ml)
water

Grease deep 20cm-round cake pan, line base with baking paper. Place whole oranges in medium saucepan; cover oranges with hot water. Bring to a boil; reduce heat, simmer, covered, about 2 hours or until oranges are tender. Replenish water with boiling water as it evaporates. Drain oranges, cool; discard water. Preheat oven to moderately slow. **Blend** or process almonds and sugar until almonds are chopped coarsely; transfer mixture to medium bowl.
Quarter whole oranges, discard seeds; blend or process until smooth. With motor operating, add eggs one at a time, process until combined. Add almond mixture, baking powder and essence; process until just combined. Spread mixture into prepared pan; bake in moderately slow oven about 1 hour.
Pour hot Lime Syrup over hot cake in pan. Stand cake in pan for 30 minutes. Turn cake onto wire rack over tray. Serve warm or cold with caramelised orange and lime rind, if desired.
Lime Syrup Combine ingredients in small saucepan; stir over heat, without boiling, until sugar dissolves. Simmer, uncovered, without stirring, about 5 minutes or until slightly thickened.

SERVES 8
Per serving 20.6g fat; 1713kJ

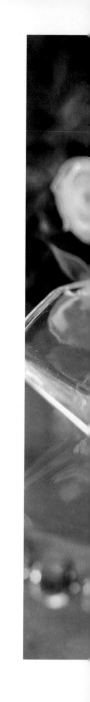

56 double chocolate
brownies

125g unsalted butter

2 cups (300g) dark chocolate Melts

1½ cups (330g) caster sugar

3 eggs, beaten lightly

¾ cup (110g) plain flour

¼ cup (35g) self-raising flour

⅓ cup (35g) cocoa powder

white chocolate fudge

60g butter

2½ cups (375g) white chocolate Melts, chopped finely

400g can (300ml) sweetened condensed milk

1 tablespoon Amaretto

Preheat oven to moderate. Grease 23cm-square slab cake pan, line base and two opposite sides with baking paper, extending paper 2cm above edge of pan.

Melt butter in medium saucepan, stir in chocolate. Stir over low heat until smooth. Transfer to large bowl. Stir in sugar and eggs. Stir in sifted flours and cocoa. Spread into prepared pan. Bake in moderate oven about 35 minutes. Cool in pan. Top brownie with White Chocolate Fudge, cover; refrigerate until firm. Dust with a little sifted icing sugar and cocoa, if desired.

White Chocolate Fudge Melt butter in medium saucepan over low heat. Stir in chocolate, milk and liqueur; cook, stirring, until smooth.

MAKES 16
Per serving 26.7g fat; 2170kJ

We used Granny Smith apples in this recipe.

2 large apples (400g), peeled, chopped finely

1 cup (200g) finely chopped seeded dates

1 teaspoon bicarbonate of soda

1 cup (250ml) boiling water

125g butter

1 teaspoon vanilla essence

1 cup (220g) caster sugar

1 egg

1½ cups (225g) plain flour

topping

60g butter

½ cup (100g) firmly packed brown sugar

½ cup (125ml) milk

⅔ cup (50g) shredded coconut

Preheat oven to moderate. Grease 23cm-square slab cake pan, line base with baking paper.

Combine apple, dates, soda and the water in medium bowl; cover, stand 10 minutes.

Meanwhile, beat butter, essence, sugar and egg in small bowl with electric mixer until light and fluffy. Transfer mixture to large bowl, stir in apple mixture and flour; pour into prepared pan.

Bake in moderate oven 50 minutes; spread with Topping, bake further 20 minutes. Stand cake 5 minutes; turn onto wire rack to cool.

Topping Combine ingredients in small saucepan, stir over low heat until butter is melted and ingredients combined.

SERVES 16
Per serving 12.4g fat; 1103kJ

58 black forest

torte

We used a packet cake mix that does not call for butter to be added; you do not need to use the ingredients listed on the packet.

370g packet rich chocolate cake mix

60g butter

2 eggs

1/3 cup (80ml) buttermilk

1/2 cup (120g) sour cream

60g dark chocolate, melted

1/4 cup (60ml) Kirsch

900ml thickened cream

cherry filling

2 x 425g cans seeded black cherries

1 1/2 tablespoons cornflour

Preheat oven to moderate. Grease deep 23cm-round cake pan, line base with baking paper.
Beat cake mix, butter, eggs, buttermilk, sour cream and cooled chocolate in small bowl with electric mixer on low speed until combined. Beat on medium speed 2 minutes or until mixture has changed to a lighter colour.
Spread cake mixture into prepared pan; bake in moderate oven about 50 minutes. Stand cake in pan 5 minutes; turn onto wire rack to cool.
Split cold cake horizontally into three layers; place one layer on serving plate, brush with some of the liqueur. Spread cake layer with half the cold Cherry Filling and a quarter of the whipped cream; top with a second layer.
Repeat layering with remaining liqueur, Filling and another quarter of the whipped cream, finishing with the third cake layer. Decorate cake with remaining half of whipped cream; refrigerate 3 hours.
Cherry Filling Drain cherries over jug, reserve 2/3 cup (160ml) syrup. Chop cherries roughly. Combine blended cornflour and syrup with cherries in small saucepan; stir over heat until mixture boils and thickens; cover, cool.

SERVES 10
Per serving 49.7g fat; 2745kJ

glossary

almonds

blanched: skins removed.

flaked: paper-thin slices.

kernels: natural kernels with skin.

meal: also known as finely ground almonds; almonds powdered to a flour-like texture.

slivered: small lengthways-cut pieces.

amaretto an almond-flavoured liqueur.

baking powder raising agent consisting mainly of two parts cream of tartar to one part bicarbonate of soda.

bicarbonate of soda also known as baking or carb soda.

biscuits also known as cookies.

butter use salted or unsalted ("sweet") butter; 125g is equal to one stick of butter.

buttermilk commercially made (by a method similar to yogurt) milk that is low in fat, with 1.8g fat per 100ml.

cheese

cottage: unripened curd cheese; we used a low-fat variety with 2g fat per 100g.

cream: commonly known as "Philadelphia" or "Philly"; soft milk cheese with 33g fat per 100g.

mascarpone: thick, triple-cream cheese with sweet, slightly sour taste.

ricotta: a sweet curd cheese. We used a low-fat variety with 8.5g fat per 100g.

chocolate

choc bits: also known as chocolate chips and chocolate morsels; available in milk, white and dark chocolate. These hold their shape in baking and are ideal for decorating.

dark: eating chocolate; made of sugar, cocoa butter and cocoa liquor (solids).

melts: available in milk, white and dark chocolate; good for melting and moulding.

white: eating chocolate, basically cocoa butter without any cocoa liquor (solids), sugar and milk.

coconut

desiccated: unsweetened, concentrated, dried, shredded coconut.

flaked: flaked and dried coconut flesh.

shredded: thin strips of dried coconut flesh.

cornflour also known as cornstarch; used as a thickening agent in cooking.

cream also known as pure cream and pouring cream. Contains a minimum fat content of 35% and has no additives, unlike thickened cream.

sour: a thick, commercially cultured, soured cream with a minimum fat content of 35%; has sharp, tangy taste.

thickened: a whipping cream (minimum fat content 35%) containing a thickener.

essence also known as extracts; generally the by-product of distillation of plants.

fillo pastry also known as phyllo dough; comes in tissue-thin sheets, bought chilled or frozen.

flour

plain: an all-purpose flour, made from wheat.

self-raising: plain flour sifted with baking powder in the ratio of 1 cup flour to 2 level teaspoons of baking powder.

ghee clarified butter.

golden syrup a by-product of refined sugarcane; pure maple syrup or honey can be substituted.

grand marnier orange-flavoured liqueur.

hazelnut meal also known as finely ground hazelnuts; hazelnuts ground to powdery, flour-like texture.

kahlua coffee-flavoured liqueur.

kirsch cherry-flavoured liqueur.

maple syrup distilled sap of the maple tree. Maple-Flavoured Syrup or pancake syrup is not an adequate substitute.

milk we used full-cream homogenised milk.

sweetened condensed: a canned product consisting of milk with more than half the water content removed and sugar added to the milk that remains.

mixed dried fruit mixture of sultanas, raisins, currants, mixed peel and cherries.

mixed peel candied citrus peel.

mixed spice a ground-spice blend of allspice, cinnamon and nutmeg.

oil, vegetable oils that have been sourced from a variety of plants rather than animal fats.

panettone a tall, cylindrical sweet bread containing sultanas and peel. Can be purchased from delicatessens and some supermarkets, particularly around Christmas time.

quince large, yellow-skinned, fragrant fruit with crunchy cream flesh that, when slow-cooked, turns a deep ruby-red in colour.

rhubarb is a vegetable and only the firm, reddish stems are eaten; the leaves are toxic.

sugar we used coarse granulated table sugar, also known as crystal sugar, unless otherwise specified.

brown: a soft, fine sugar retaining molasses.

caster: also called superfine or finely granulated sugar.

icing sugar mixture: also known as confectioners' sugar or powdered sugar; granulated sugar crushed together with small amount of added cornflour.

sultanas dried grapes, also known as golden raisins.

tia maria coffee-flavoured liqueur.

vanilla bean dried long, thin pod from a tropical orchid; the tiny black seeds inside the bean impart a vanilla flavour.

62

index